The Magna Carta Trivia Challenge

Jonathan Ozanne

DEDICATION

For Sarah, Josiah, Gideon, and Samuel

In memory of Micah.

CONTENTS

ACKNOWLEDGMENTS

The author is grateful for the encouragement he has
received from his family
and friends while writing this book.

About the cover: The cover is a stylized representation of
the Magna Carta as a strong tower of English law. The
white on the cover represents the new beginning that the
Magna Carta was for English law and law in general.
Three gold lions on a red field became the symbol of the
Royal Banner of England in 1198, shortly before the
creation of the Magna Carta. Thus, the Royal Banner is a
relevant symbol to include to represent England. The
banner for the cover was created with the software
program Campaign Cartographer 3 by Profantasy
Software, Ltd.

INTRODUCTION

The Magna Carta is an important document. It is old and historic, yet at the same time it is alive and well in the world today as a symbol of liberty. It is celebrated in many countries that have a strong English legal heritage, most notably the United Kingdom, the Commonwealth nations, and the United States of America.

This book presents a series of questions about the Magna Carta and some of the major milestones in history that have come from it. The answers are in the back. The answers often go into greater detail about the Magna Carta. You can read this book alone or with a group. If you are reading this book with a group you can compete to see who gets the most answers correct or you can cooperate as a team.

I hope you have as much fun answering these questions as I had researching and writing them! Thank you for buying this book.

Jonathan Ozanne

QUESTIONS

AT THE TIME OF THE MAGNA CARTA

To better understand the Magna Carta, it is important to know what was happening when it came into being. This section explores what was happening in England and what had happened under the reign of King John leading up to the Magna Carta.

1. When was the Magna Carta agreed upon?
    - A. 1215
    - B. 1635
    - C. 1865

2. Where was the Magna Carta formally agreed upon?
    - A. Dover
    - B. Portsmouth
    - C. Runnymede

3. Who was the Magna Carta directed at?
    - A. King John
    - B. King Richard
    - C. Robin Hood

4. Who imposed the Magna Carta on the king?
    - A. His barons
    - B. The Pope
    - C. The serfs

5. Why was the Magna Carta imposed on King John?
    A. To restrain his abuses of power
    B. Historians still do not know why
    C. As revenge for the Haymarket incident

6. Which of the following was one of the reasons that King John agreed to the Magna Carta?
    A. To end a civil war
    B. To get more concessions from the nobility
    C. To celebrate the rights of humankind

7. Did Parliament exist at the time of the creation of the Magna Carta?
    A. Yes
    B. No

8. Although taxes are seldom popular, which of the following taxes was very unpopular at the time of the Magna Carta?
    A. Inheritance Taxes
    B. Income Taxes
    C. Sales Taxes

9. Based on his heavy-handed taxation policies, King John was very successful in raising money from his subjects and making them angry. What percentage of the currency in England was in John's treasury at the height of his reign?
   A. Approximately 10%
   B. Approximately 30%
   C. Approximately 50%

10. At the time of the Magna Carta, generally the currency of England was made out of what metal?
    A. Gold
    B. Tin
    C. Silver

11. What was King John's favorite hobby?
    A. Falconry
    B. Jousting
    C. Racquetball

ENGLISH LAW PRIOR TO
THE MAGNA CARTA

Many casual legal histories give the impression that
before the Magna Carta there was no law. Obviously
this is an exaggeration. The questions in this next
section examine developments in and the general
state of English law prior to the Magna Carta. These
questions will provide a context for understanding the
importance of the Magna Carta.

12. Which of the following English kings was a
    strong proponent of the concept of the rule
    of law?
    A. Alfred the Great
    B. Ethelred the Unready
    C. Wulfstan the Mighty

13. What written work did King Henry I help
    create that provided a memorable legal
    precedent for future generations?
    A. His Coronation Charter of Liberties
    B. His multi-volume legal treatise
    C. His best-selling legal thriller novel

14. King Henry II issued the Constitution of Claredon (1164). What important right did that document formally grant?
    A. The right to a jury trial
    B. The right to legal counsel at trial
    C. The right to a speedy trial

15. What type of trial was the setting for the important right (the subject of the previous question) granted in the Constitution of Claredon (1164)?
    A. Trial by ordeal
    B. Trial by the King's Bench
    C. Trial by church court

16. Which of the following kings was widely considered by his subjects to be a just ruler?
    A. Albert the Proud
    B. Edward the Confessor
    C. Richard the Lionheart

17. According to the Constitution of Claredon (1164), how many jurors should be on a jury?
    A. The number of jurors is not addressed in that law
    B. 9
    C. 12

TEXT OF THE MAGNA CARTA

These questions are about what is actually written in the Magna Carta of 1215. Interpretation questions are found in later sections that explore the legacy of the Magna Carta.

18. What does "Magna Carta" mean?
    A. Small law
    B. Great charter
    C. Splendid law

19. In what language was the Magna Carta written?
    A. English
    B. French
    C. Latin

20. Is there any punctuation in the text of the Magna Carta as originally written?
    A. Yes
    B. No

21. The Magna Carta of 1215 has subsequently been divided into 63 chapters. Many chapters are only one or two sentences long. Which of the following answers best describes the subject of the first chapter?
    A. Administration of justice
    B. Feudal estates
    C. Religious freedom

22. Starting with chapter 2 of the Magna Carta of 1215, the next group of chapters are about what topic of major concern for the barons?
    A. Administration of justice
    B. Feudal estates
    C. Free trade

23. Starting with chapter 17 of the Magna Carta of 1215, the third group of chapters deals with what topic of major concern for the barons?
    A. Administration of justice
    B. Feudal estates
    C. Free trade

24. Does the Magna Carta favor free trade?
    A. Yes
    B. No

25. Which of the following issues is addressed in the most detail by the Magna Carta?
    A. Castles
    B. Crusades
    C. Taxes

26. The Magna Carta has a chapter about fishing on the Thames river. What does it say about such fishing?
    A. The fishing weirs must be removed from the river
    B. The fishing weirs must be put back in the river
    C. No spear fishing

27. Which country does the Magna Carta have favorable terms towards in an effort to get the people of that country to support the barons?
    A. Cornwall
    B. Germany
    C. Wales

28. The king of which of the following countries was loyal to King John at the time of the Magna Carta and was specifically mentioned in the Magna Carta?
   A. Germany
   B. Scotland
   C. Wales

29. Did King John sign the Magna Carta or just place his royal seal on it?
   A. Royal seal only
   B. Signed it

30. Did the Magna Carta create Parliament as we know it today?
   A. Yes, the council of barons, created in the last chapters of the Magna Carta, was very similar in form and purpose to the modern Parliament
   B. No, although the Magna Carta offered some early hints at the possibility of a Parliament, it did not create Parliament

ENGLISH LAW AFTER THE MAGNA CARTA

This section explores the legacy of the Magna Carta on English legal history. The questions focus on developments in English law that can be traced back to the Magna Carta.

31. True or False? The original Magna Carta was nullified by the Pope at the request of King John?

32. What was one of the first acts of King Henry III (reign 1217 to 1272)?
    A. To further repudiate the Magna Carta as a worthless scrap of parchment
    B. To confirm a reissued Magna Carta and swear to uphold it

33. What happened in 1225?
    A. Parliament was officially established
    B. The Magna Carta was reissued with a reissue of the Charter of the Forest
    C. The Charter of London was issued

34. What happened in 1237?
    A. The Magna Carta was repudiated
    B. Civil war broke out
    C. The Magna Carta was confirmed again

35. What did King Edward I do in 1297?
   A. He enrolled the Magna Carta as a statute
   B. He repudiated the Magna Carta as a dusty old law
   C. He significantly abrogated the Magna Carta

36. How many times was the Magna Carta confirmed by kings in the 200 years after 1215?
   A. 0
   B. At least 40 times
   C. At least 100 times

37. What happened from 1472 to 1628?
   A. The Magna Carta was not mentioned in any of the statutes that were enacted during that span of time
   B. The Magna Carta was only mentioned three times in statutes that were enacted during that span of time
   C. The Magna Carta was mentioned well over 700 times in statutes that were enacted during that span of time

38. What major legal phrase was first recorded in a statute in 1354?
    A. Double jeopardy
    B. Due process of law
    C. Speedy trial

39. Which of the following legal concepts is hinted at in the Magna Carta but would take a few more centuries to develop?
    A. Corpus Callosum
    B. Corpus Delicti
    C. Habeas Corpus

40. Which author wrote a major work of legal history called *Institutes of the Laws of England*?
    A. William Blackstone
    B. Edward Coke
    C. Thomas Hobbes

41. Which author wrote a major work of legal history called *Commentaries on the Laws of England* as well as the first modern history book on the Magna Carta?
    A. William Blackstone
    B. Edward Coke
    C. John Locke

42. Which author held the post of attorney general for King James I and was influential in the drafting of many of the American colonial charters?
   A. Edward Coke
   B. Thomas Hobbes
   C. John Locke

43. Due to the work of people like Edward Coke, what has the Magna Carta symbolized for centuries?
   A. The good of the one outweighs the good of the few or the many
   B. Even kings must bow before the law
   C. The wonderful power of an absolute monarchy

44. Which of the following issues was settled by the Petition of Right (1628)?
   A. Consent of Parliament is required for taxes
   B. Consent of Parliament is required for abrogation of free speech rights
   C. Voting rights belong to the people

45. True or False. When William and Mary were crowned king and queen in 1689 the Magna Carta was incorporated into the Coronation Oath of the new monarchy?

46. Which answer best describes the role of the Magna Carta in English law from 1215 to 1450?
    A. It provided an actual legal framework for many areas of law
    B. It provided an inspirational framework for new ideas
    C. It was not so important to English law at this time

47. Which answer best describes the role of the Magna Carta in English law from 1450 to 1600?
    A. It provided an actual legal framework for many areas of law
    B. It provided an inspirational framework for new ideas
    C. It was not so important to English law at this time

48. Which answer best describes the role of the Magna Carta in English law from 1600 to 2000?
    A. It provided an actual legal framework for many areas of law
    B. It provided an inspirational framework for new ideas
    C. It was not so important to English law at this time

49. How many chapters of the Magna Carta are still valid law today in 2015?
    A. 3
    B. 8
    C. 17

50. The enduring law from the Magna Carta has been what kind of law?
    A. Due process law
    B. Feudal tenure law
    C. Inheritance tax law

One of the greatest exports in the history of the United Kingdom and the British Empire is the rule of law found in the Magna Carta

THE MAGNA CARTA HISTORIC SITES

This section has questions about some of the places in England that are linked to the Magna Carta, often because there is at least one surviving ancient copy of the Magna Carta from the 13th century at that location.

51. Which city was captured by the rebellious barons shortly before the Magna Carta was sealed at Runnymede?
    A. Bath
    B. Dover
    C. London

52. True or False. The rebellious barons sometimes met at churches when plotting what to do about King John?

53. Which of the following cities has three copies of the Magna Carta from the 13th century?
    A. Durham
    B. Hereford
    C. Nottingham

54. The best surviving original copy of the
    Magna Carta is found near the tallest spire in
    England and is located in which city?
    - A. Birmingham
    - B. Salisbury
    - C. Southampton

55. Which city has a copy of the Magna Carta
    that survived the ravages of the English Civil
    War but was sent to the United States for
    safekeeping during World War II?
    - A. Lincoln
    - B. Portsmouth
    - C. Torquay

56. Which of the following cities has a copy of
    the Magna Carta that was issued in 1217?
    - A. Hereford
    - B. Lancaster
    - C. Liverpool

57. How many copies of the 1217 edition of the
    Magna Carta are found at Oxford?
    - A. 0
    - B. 2
    - C. 3

58. How many copies of the original version of the Magna Carta (1215) still survive?
    A. 4
    B. 8
    C. 12

"No freeman shall be taken or imprisoned or disseised of any freehold, or liberties, or free customs, or outlawed, or banished, or in any other way destroyed, nor will we go upon him, nor send upon him, except by the legal judgment of his peers or by the law of the land. To no one will we sell, to no one will we deny, or delay right or justice."

- The Magna Carta (1215), chapters 39, 40
- The Magna Carta (1225), chapter 29

LAWS INSPIRED BY THE MAGNA CARTA

This section focuses on how the Magna Carta
inspired developments in the laws of other countries.

59. How was the Magna Carta exported to other
   lands?
   - A. Wandering scribes took copies of
     the Magna Carta around the world
     in the 15th century
   - B. Embassy space was leased in the
     Tower of London and foreign
     officials had a chance to see the
     Magna Carta on the way to work
     each day
   - C. The colonies of the British Empire
     inherited many customs from Britain
     including a common legal heritage

60. Which author was highly influential on
   American understanding of the history of the
   Magna Carta and his writings helped export
   the ideas of the Magna Carta to the United
   States?
   - A. Edward Coke
   - B. Thomas Hobbes
   - C. John Locke

61. Which of the following rights from the Bill of Rights in the United States Constitution can be traced back to the Magna Carta?
    A. Free speech
    B. Jury trial
    C. Right to bear arms

62. Which of the following ideals has the Magna Carta come to symbolize?
    A. I am the state
    B. Limited government
    C. No taxation without representation

63. Including amendments, how many due process clauses are in the United States Constitution?
    A. 0
    B. 1
    C. 2

64. Why has the Bill of Rights in the United States Constitution and the Bills of Rights found in various state constitutions been so successful at protecting liberty?
    A. Coincidence
    B. People have worked hard to achieve these aspirational goals
    C. The rights in these Bills of Rights represent rights that were already protected at common law

65. True or False. Most Commonwealth nations have language from the Magna Carta in their respective constitutions?

66. True or False. The United Nations Universal Declaration of Human Rights (1948) was inspired by the Magna Carta?

ANSWERS

Throughout the answers references to the Magna Carta in **bold** refer to the chapters of the 1225 text. References to the Magna Carta in [brackets] refer to the 1215 text. Example (see chapter **29**, [39, 40])

AT THE TIME OF THE MAGNA CARTA

1. A. The Magna Carta was agreed upon in 1215. It was formally agreed to on the 15th of June, 1215.

2. C. The Magna Carta was agreed upon at Runnymede. Runnymede is located along the Thames River, near London and Windsor.

3. A. The Magna Carta was directed at King John.

4. A. The Magna Carta was imposed by his barons who were in revolt against him. Robert fitz Walter (1180-1235) was the leader of the barons.

5. A. The Magna Carta was imposed on King John to restrain his abuses of power.

6. A. King John agreed to the demands of the barons to end a civil war. Only a month before the barons had captured London and

John's military position was not good. Continuing the civil war would likely have resulted in John being deposed. John was smart enough to make a deal to avoid or at least delay a potentially disastrous war.

7. B. No. Parliament did not exist at the time of the Magna Carta.

8. A. Inheritance taxes were raised considerably under King John. These were taxes that were paid in order to receive an inheritance. The inheritance taxes were used in a more punitive and political fashion by the greedy and ruthless John. Normally the inheritance tax was high but the person who would inherit was given plenty of time to pay off the tax. John raised the taxes and started seizing the lands of people who could not pay fast enough. The Magna Carta worked to correct these excesses by undoing changes to the law made by John. The Magna Carta also set monetary limits on the tax.

9. C. It has been estimated that King John obtained close to 30 million silver pennies at the height of his reign. This represented about half of the money in circulation at the time. Between fighting wars in France and his own luxurious lifestyle he managed to

spend almost all of the money that he accumulated.

10. C. Generally English currency of the time was made out of silver.

11. A. King John's favorite hobby was falconry. Falconry is an expensive sport that involves hunting with highly trained birds of prey. It was a popular sport for the nobility during the Middle Ages.

ENGLISH LAW PRIOR TO THE MAGNA CARTA

12. A. King Alfred the Great (the only English king to be known as "the Great", reign from 871 to 901) was a strong proponent of the rule of law and a system of justice based on laws rather than men.

13. A. King Henry I had a Coronation Charter of Liberties, often referred to as either the Coronation Charter or the Charter of Liberties. His charter provided a precedent and inspiration for future generations. The precedent was that the king promised to rule as a good king. The Coronation Charter of Liberties provided some inspiration for the Magna Carta, namely the idea that the king could be made to promise good

behavior and to rule justly in exchange for loyalty from his subjects. At first the barons wanted John to merely confirm the Charter of Liberties (1100) but they later demanded that John agree to a new charter – the Magna Carta.

14. A. The Constitution of Claredon (1164) formally granted the right to a jury trial.

15. C. The right to a jury trial was granted for a church trial in an ecclesiastical court. Slowly over the centuries, the right to a jury trial moved into trials held in civil and criminal courts.

16. B. Edward the Confessor was thought to be a just king. He was cited favorably by his successors as a model king that the successors wished to emulate.

17. C. 12 jurors are on a jury according to the Constitution of Claredon (1164).

TEXT OF THE MAGNA CARTA

18. B. The phrase "Magna Carta" means "great charter" in Latin.

19. C. The Magna Carta was written in Latin.

20. B. No. The Magna Carta as written is not punctuated or divided into clauses or chapters. Later printers, such as Tottell, added the convention of dividing it into chapters to aid in reading the charter.

21. C. The first section of the Magna Carta deals with religious freedom of the institutional church. The language of the chapter is very broad. It is possible that the Archbishop of Canterbury, Stephen Langton, who helped mediate the negotiations between the barons and John, influenced the contents of this first chapter. (See chapter **1**, [1])

22. B. The second section of the Magna Carta deals with feudal estates. To finance his territorial ambitions in France, King John raised taxes and seized assets of people who did not pay fast enough. The Magna Carta limited those taxes and reduced the harsh penalties. (See chapters **2 through 10**, **31**, **32**, **33**, **36**, **37** [2 through 10, 11, 14, 15, 16, 25, 37, 43, 46])

23. A. The third section of the Magna Carta deals with the administration of justice. This section includes the due process requirements that the Magna Carta is famous for and also includes changes to administration of the royal forests. These laws all work to keep justice fair and reduce arbitrariness in the legal process. (See chapters **11 through 22**, **24**, **26 through 29**, **34**, **35** [17 through 24, 26 through 32, 34, 36, 38, 39, 40, 44, 45, 47, 48, 52, 53, 54, 55])

24. A. Yes. The Magna Carta favors free trade. Foreign merchants are to be allowed into England without penalty unless English merchants are being mistreated abroad. (See chapters **30** [41, 42])

25. C. All three answer choices are addressed by the Magna Carta but of the three taxes are dealt with in the most detail and the most chapters by the Magna Carta. (See chapters **2**, **3**, **7**, **20**, **31**, **32**, **37** [2, 3, 7, 8, 12, 14, 15, 25, 29, 43, 53, 60])

26. A. The fishing weirs must be removed from the river. These solid fish traps constituted a navigation hazard. (See chapter **23** [33])

27. C. At the time of Magna Carta, the barons sought Welsh aid against King John and the Magna Carta includes a few chapters that are an attempt to win Welsh support for the barons. For example, the relevant chapters offer greater justice to the Welsh and to undo wrongs that previous kings had done to the Welsh. (See chapters [49, 56, 57, 58])

28. B. The King of Scotland, Andrew, was an ally of King John. King Andrew was an ally because King John helped Andrew obtain the Scottish throne. There is a chapter in the Magna Carta that attempts to convince the Scots to support the barons but the Scots remained supporters of John. (See chapter [59])

29. A. King John only placed his royal seal on it (the Great Seal). He did not actually sign his name. The royal seal was sufficient to make the document legal and binding.

30. B. No. Although the Magna Carta offers hints of a future Parliament through two chapters that can be interpreted to say something about taxation only with representation and a chapter about the council of barons (a group of 25 barons assigned by the 1215 Magna Carta to help

oversee implementation of the charter), it did not create Parliament. (See chapters [12, 14, 61])

ENGLISH LAW AFTER THE MAGNA CARTA

31. True. The original Magna Carta was nullified by Pope Innocent III within a few months, at the request of King John. John had hoped that the Magna Carta would be turned into an empty pledge but the barons were determined to force him to comply with the terms. The barons were not blameless in the breakdown; it was not 100% John's fault. Finding this arrangement to be unacceptable, John appealed to Pope Innocent III to overturn the Magna Carta. This was also a noteworthy turn of events because John had spent many years of his reign feuding with the Pope and had been excommunicated for a time. However, John had made peace with Rome and in return the Pope had nullified the original Magna Carta. John may have deceived the Pope by promising to go on a crusade. John's status as a crusader was cited by the Pope in his order (papal bull) nullifying the original Magna Carta.

32. B. After the Magna Carta was nullified, a renewed civil war broke out. It ended when King John died of dysentery in October of 1216 and the barons were willing to recognize John's son Henry III as the next king. One of the first acts of Henry III's reign was to confirm a hastily reissued Magna Carta and to swear to uphold it. As Henry III was not yet of legal age, this act was done on his behalf by the regent, William Marshall, 4th Earl of Pembroke.

33. B. In 1225 the Magna Carta and the Charter of the Forest were reissued by Henry III (now of legal age) in exchange for a onetime tax. The Charter of the Forest contained many laws from the original Magna Carta that had been reissued as a separate law in 1217 after the first Magna Carta had been invalidated. The Charter of the Forest helped protect people from arbitrary penalties and other injustices with the laws concerning the royal forests.

34. C. Showing that the Magna Carta was an important law, in 1237 Henry III again confirmed the Magna Carta as the law of the land.

35. A. In 1297 Edward I reissued the Magna Carta. This reissue was known as the

inspeximus. As part of the reissue the *Magna Carta de Libertatibus Angliae* (Great Charter of the Liberties of England) was added to the Statute Roll giving it the force of law of a statute. It further shows the highly elevated status of the Magna Carta that 80 years later it was still considered to be a significant law. Portions of the Magna Carta from 1225 are still valid law.

36. B. The Magna Carta was confirmed at least 40 times in the next 200 years. It remained a cornerstone of English law. The promise to uphold the Magna Carta replaced the promise to follow the good laws of Edward the Confessor.

37. A. For roughly 150 years from 1472 to 1628, the Magna Carta was not mentioned in the statutes.

38. B. The phrase "due process of law" is associated with the Magna Carta but that phrase did not actually appear in a statute until 1354. The Magna Carta clearly provides a solid foundation for the concept of due process of law even though it never uses that exact phrase.

39. C. Habeas Corpus is a writ which compels the production of a person and is now used

by defendants to challenge their incarceration. Originally the writ was used to procure witnesses or to move the case from an inferior court to a superior one. Habeas Corpus did not fully develop until the late 1600s, particularly with the 1679 Habeas Corpus Act. The Magna Carta contained several medieval writs which helped advance the criminal law from legally sanctioned dueling to the advanced legal system of today.

40. B. Sir Edward Coke (pronounced Cook) wrote a major work of English legal history called *Institutes on the Laws of England*. Coke was a tremendous legal scholar. He served as a judge before being dismissed by James I. Coke wrote about the supremacy of the common law. Common law is law made by judges in the course of deciding a case.

41. A. Writing in the 1750s and 1760s (about a century and a quarter after Coke) was Sir William Blackstone. He wrote a legal history of England that is known as the *Commentaries on the Laws of England*, often shortened to the *Commentaries*. He also wrote a history of the Magna Carta (*The Great Charter and the Charter of the Forest*) that clarified many details that were

unknown at the time. Early chroniclers of the Magna Carta were not aware of the distinctions between the 1215, 1216, 1217, and 1225 versions. Blackstone explained these differences.

42. A. Sir Edward Coke as attorney general for the Crown (serving King James I) was influential in drafting the Virginia Charter. Both Coke's *Institutes* and his work on colonial charters were highly influential on the development of American law.

43. B. Edward Coke wrote a history of the Magna Carta and the struggle with the tyranny of John. As a judge on the King's Bench he stood up to the tyranny of James I and was removed from his post. Coke died in 1634 (while Charles I was still king) but Coke's work inspired the continuing struggle against the tyranny of Charles I and inspired the Americans in their opposition to George III.

44. A. In response to the tyranny of Charles I, Parliament, with the Petition of Right, established that the consent of Parliament is required before the king can impose taxes.

45. True. The Magna Carta was incorporated into the Coronation Oath used by William and Mary in 1689. In the 1688 Coronation Act, the Coronation Oath was revised to include all the statutes, laws, and customs of Parliament, which included the Magna Carta which had been enrolled as a statute since 1297.

46. A. From approximately 1215 to 1450 the Magna Carta was important for English law because it provided an actual framework for many areas of law, including free trade, procedural law, and feudal tenures.

47. C. From approximately 1450 to 1600 the Magna Carta was not so important to English law. It faded into the background because it began to be superseded by other laws (although it was not expressly overruled during this time) and more of its provisions became obsolete as time marched on and England advanced out of the Middle Ages.

48. B. Although it had faded, it was not forgotten. From approximately 1600 to 2000 the Magna Carta was an important source of inspiration for those who wished to promote liberty. This inspiration began with those confronting the tyranny of

Charles I (reign 1625-1649). The text of the Magna Carta was reinterpreted in a 17th century context to view the Magna Carta as a bulwark of individual rights against arbitrary government action by a different king determined to be a tyrant. This reimagining of the Magna Carta led to the laws that are collectively known as the English Constitution. The English Constitution works to protect individual rights. Even today, for many people around the world, the Magna Carta remains an inspiration of liberty.

49. A. Three chapters of the Magna Carta are still valid law today. They include the chapter on religious freedom (**1**), the chapter protecting the rights of towns (**9**), and the most famous chapter of the Magna Carta, the one protecting due process rights (**29**). The chapters refer to the 1225 text because that text was used when the Magna Carta was enrolled as a statute in 1297.

50. A. The enduring law from the Magna Carta has been due process law. Due process law provides a check against arbitrary exercise of government power.

THE MAGNA CARTA HISTORIC SITES

51. C. London was captured by the barons shortly before the Magna Carta was sealed at Runnymede. The capture of London helped to force the confrontation with King John. The barons installed a new mayor when they captured London.

52. True. The rebellious barons sometimes met at churches to plot about how to deal with the tyranny of King John. Some places that they met included the St. Albans Abbey at St. Albans, and at the Abbey Church at Bury St. Edmunds.

53. A. Durham has three copies of the Magna Carta, including ones from 1216, 1225, and 1300. Durham has the only surviving version of the Magna Carta from 1216.

54. B. The best surviving original copy of the Magna Carta is on public display at St. Mary's Cathedral in Salisbury. The Salisbury Cathedral has the tallest spire in England.

55. A. The 1215 copy of the Magna Carta found in Lincoln survived the ravages of the English Civil War but was sent to the United States for safekeeping during World War II.

56. A. Hereford has a copy of the Magna Carta that was issued in 1217.

57. C. Three copies of the 1217 edition of the Magna Carta are found in Oxford.

58. A. Four copies of the original 1215 Magna Carta still survive. One copy is at the Lincoln Cathedral, one is at the Salisbury Cathedral and two copies are at the British Library.

LAWS INSPIRED BY THE MAGNA CARTA

59. C. The colonies of the British Empire inherited many customs from Britain including a common legal heritage. Among the countries with a common legal heritage with the United Kingdom are Australia, Canada, Ghana, India, Kenya, New Zealand, Pakistan, and the United States.

60. A. Coke's history of the Magna Carta was highly influential on American understanding of the history of the Magna Carta. Coke's history views the Magna Carta through his perspective on the turmoil of the 17th century and the tyranny of James I. Not surprisingly, Coke's work found a ready audience as the American colonies feuded with Britain and George III.

61. B. The right to a jury trial can be traced back to the Magna Carta. The Magna Carta does not literally grant the right to a jury trial. However, it does include the right to a feudal jury for determining a type of forfeiture penalty, and the right to be punished only after the judgment of peers. These rights formed the basis for the right to a jury trial and are why the right to a jury trial is said to come from Magna Carta. The other rights mentioned in the question (free speech and bear arms) are not in the Magna Carta. (See chapters **20**, **29** [20-22, 39, 40])

62. B. The Magna Carta is a symbol of limited government. It is a symbol of the rule of law and that without law there cannot be freedom.

63. C. There are two due process clauses in the United States constitution. They are found in the Fifth and Fourteenth amendments. The due process clauses of the United States Constitution can be traced back to the Magna Carta and the famous chapter **29**.

64. C. The rights in the Bills of Rights (the first ten amendments to the Constitution, and the various state Bills of Rights) represent rights that were already protected at common law. Rather than aspirational goals, these rights represent established traditions that were given greater force of law. That the rights were already established helped make the Bills of Rights so successful at protecting liberty.

65. True. Most Commonwealth nations have language from the Magna Carta in their respective constitutions. One of the greatest exports in the history of the United Kingdom and the British Empire is the rule of law found in the Magna Carta.

66. True. The United Nations Universal Declaration of Human Rights (1948) was inspired by the Magna Carta. Article 9 "No one shall be subjected to arbitrary arrest, detention, or exile." Article 10 "Everyone is entitled in full equality to a fair and public hearing by an independent and impartial tribunal, in the determination of his rights and obligations and of any criminal charge against him."

SCORING

Given the difficulty of the questions, generally more than 50% correct is a good score.

Regardless of how many you got correct, I hope these questions were fun and prompt you to learn more about the Magna Carta!

BIBLIOGRAPHY AND SUGGESTED RESOURCES

American Council of Learned Societies, The. *The Great Charter: Four essays on Magna Carta and the history of our liberty*. New York : Pantheon Books, 1965.

Cannon, John and Griffiths, Ralph. *The Oxford illustrated history of the British Monarchy*. Oxford : Oxford University Press, 1992.

Castor, Helen. *She-Wolves : the women who ruled England before Elizabeth*. New York : HarperCollins Publishers, 2011.

Cormack, Patrick. *Castles of Britain*. New York : Crescent Books, 1982.

Daugherty, James. *The Magna Carta*. San Luis Obispo, CA : Beautiful Feet Books, 1956.

Fry, Plantagenet Somerset. *Kings and Queens of England and Scotland*. New York : DK Publishing, 2006.

Hamilton, J.S. *The Plantagenets : history of a dynasty*. New York : Continuum, 2010.

Heritage Foundation, The. *The Heritage Guide to the Constitution*. New York : Regnery, 2005.

Iggulden, Conn and Iggulden, David. *The dangerous book of heroes*. New York : William Morrow, 2009.

Jennings, Sir Ivor. *Magna Carta and its influence in the world today*. New York : British Information Services, 1965.

Jones, Dan. *The Plantagenets : the warrior kings and queens who made England*. New York : Viking, 2012.

Levy, Debbie. *The signing of the Magna Carta*. Minneapolis, MN : Twenty-First Century Books, 2008.

Steenson, Michael. Bench & Bar Vol. LXXII No. 1, *Roots of Constitutional Government: Magna Carta at 800*. Minneapolis, MN : Minnesota State Bar Association, 2015.

Stephenson, Carl and Marcham, Frederick George. *Sources of English Constitutional History*. New York : Harper & Brothers, Publishers, 1937.

Swindler, William F. *Magna Carta*. New York : Grosset & Dunlap, 1968.

   Magna Carta: Legend and Legacy. New York : The Bobbs-Merrill Company Inc., 1965.

Wilkinson, Philip. *The British Monarchy for Dummies*. Chichester : John Wiley & Sons, 2006.

WEBSITES

http://magnacarta800th.com

http://www.bl.uk/magna-carta/articles/magna-carta-an-introduction

http://www.legislation.gov.uk

ABOUT THE AUTHOR

The author is a lawyer who lives with his family near St. Paul, Minnesota. He is an honors graduate with a B.A. in history/political science from the University of Jamestown, Jamestown, North Dakota. He received his J.D. from the Hamline University School of Law in St. Paul, Minnesota. Some of the other quiz books he has written include: *Santa Claus's Christmas Trivia Challenge: 100 questions about the secular and sacred customs of Christmas*, *Easter Trivia Challenge* and *George Washington's Monumental Presidential Trivia Challenge : More than 500 questions about the 44 U.S. Presidents from Washington to Obama*. When not working, the author enjoys taking his sons to state parks.